Geneva Travel Guide

Sightseeing, Hotel, Restaurant
& Shopping Highlights

Amanda Morgan

Table of Contents

Geneva

Geneva is a pleasant, modern city and is a major European financial center. Located on Lake Geneva with Mont Blanc hovering in the distance, Geneva is an idyllic Swiss village at heart. It is the second-largest city in Switzerland and is an important world center of diplomacy, being home to the United Nations (UN) and the Red Cross. Geneva is also an exciting, historical, and scenic city to visit.

Head down to the lake for an afternoon swim or an evening boat cruise. Take the gondola up the Saleve, and gaze across the beautiful Swiss Alps and down to the Rhone River Valley.

The history of Geneva is typical of so many European cities: power seemed to change hands at the drop of a hat for centuries until the 19th century, when the Napoleonic Wars ended and Geneva entered the Swiss Confederation. About two thousand years ago, Geneva was a fortified town to protect the Roman Empire against Helvetii, a notoriously violent Celtic tribe in the region. The city remained under the auspices of the Holy Roman Empire for another 13 centuries, until the House of Savoy began to rule Geneva, which had been granted a large amount of self-governance.

France had taken much control of the city by the 18th century, however, the French Revolution created another opportunity for Geneva to reclaim its relative autonomy, and after Napoleon left, Geneva joined the Swiss Confederation, leading to centuries of economic stability and prosperity.

Today, Geneva is a fast-paced international financial and political center, with pockets of tiny neighborhoods where you can escape the hustle-and-bustle and enjoy food from anywhere from Afghanistan to Brazil. Head to the lake and go for a morning or afternoon jog, breathing in the crisp Swiss air, and visit impressive Cathedrals, remnants of the strong religious history Geneva has deep down in its roots.

Come to rest your weary feet from an Alpine adventure, stop off on your way to the slopes, and come for the shopping, the food, the culture, and yes, the chocolate. Haven't you heard it's the best in the world?

Culture

Most of the population of Geneva speaks French, however, interestingly; about 40% of the city's population is comprised of foreign nationals. The majority of these people use English or French in offices and in international diplomacy. There are many other languages spoken here and a great number of international eateries where you can get a taste of many other cultures.

Geneva is Switzerland's most international city, and is tucked away at the most western-edge of Switzerland near to the French border. Upon arriving, you will feel that this is a city that takes pride in its buildings, in its streets, and in its reputation.

Geneva is known as the "World's Smallest Metropolis," and many of the larger hotels are located on the right-hand shore of Lake Geneva. On the other side, you have St. Peter's Cathedral and Basilica and the Old Town, which is a charming maze of cobbled roads and small restaurants, as well as a lakeside promenade where you can enjoy an evening stroll in the fresh Swiss air.

Many people visit Geneva for business purposes but come to realize that this city is a stunning cultural attraction in its own right. It's a city to be enjoyed over an extended period of time, sipping a warm cappuccino in the crisp Alpine air, wandering through Old Town or gazing out of a glass window on the 20th story, looking out over the magical fusion of modernity and tradition that is Geneva.

Location & Orientation

Geneva is located in the western-most part of Switzerland and is an extremely accessible city. Its airport is close and convenient to the city, and is also well-served as a hub for the budget airline EasyJet for those of you choosing a thriftier way to fly.

A taxi from the airport into town won't cost very much, but you can also very easily take the number 10 bus, which leaves every 15 minutes from the airport. If you are heading to the train station, get off at stop "22-Cantons." If your destination is the UN Building, then you will want to take bus 5 instead.

Taking the train into Geneva is probably one of the most breathtaking journeys, from any direction, the mountains and heavy forests painting your windows filled with white, blue, and green. The central train station is called CFF, and is centrally-located, serving many destinations in Europe.

Getting around Geneva is very easy with the excellent tram service serving the center of city and the outskirts. You can catch the trams in front of the main train station CFF, and there are stops dispersed around the city, including many in Old Town. Once you're in Old Town, you may want to decide to explore by foot. It can get a bit hilly, but the small alleyways and boutiques are best explored slowly, window-shopping your way through the city.

Climate & When to Visit

Geneva has a fairly mild climate, but can get snow in the city itself in the colder winter months. Expect the summer months to be warm, but still a little chilly at night (that mountain air is pervasive).

July and August can be very busy, with a lot of tourists coming in to share the summer weather in the squares and around the lake, so it may be a good idea to plan your trip for June or September for slightly lower hotel rates and less crowds.

Geneva is a very popular skiing centre in wintertime with many additional flights provided at this time of year. Many ski resorts are on the city's doorstep.

Sightseeing Highlights

Lake Geneva (Boat Cruises & Swimming)

A slow-moving glacier formed Lake Geneva (also known as "Lac Léman). The lake is a crescent-moon shaped body of water that people have flocked to, for pleasure or for pillaging, for millennia. Much of the activity in Geneva, from sports to parks to nightlife, is centered on the shores of the lake. It's not a bad idea to start your visit to Geneva here, then radiate outwards.

Your first stop at the Lake should be the famous "Jet d'Eau", which is an almost 150 meter tall fountain of water, located just off the shore of the center of Geneva. Its central location between the Rhone River and Lake Geneva is purposeful: you can see this fountain from numerous places in the city, and reminds visitors of the importance of the lake to the people living here.

The water jet was built in the late 19th century, and utilizes water from Lake Geneva, which is then pumped through the nozzle at around 500 liters of water per second. For the best view, head to the pier and lighthouse in close proximity to the jet. However; be careful of the wind; sometimes it can change rapidly, and you'll be left knowing what a cool shower of lake water feels like.

Next, venture out beyond the shores and onto the lake itself on a paddleboat steamer cruise. These steamer ships, most of which were commissioned in the early 1900's, offer beautiful vistas, and a sensational panoramic view of Geneva. You can choose a variety of tours, all of which have different ports of call along the river (some of which visit the French side of the river), and even some that will tailor a tour for you.

Daily cruises head to the Lavaux Vineyards or Yvoire, a beautiful medieval town on the shores of the lake. You may even just do a two-hour cruise to gaze at the Alps and stunning natural beauty of the Lake.

For specific tour information, visit the website: http://www.cgn.ch/eng?lan=eng-GB

For a taste of the outdoors, take a bus to Nyon, which is a small town 30 minutes from Geneva International Airport. Nyon is a charming town right on the shore of Lake Geneva. It is located on the road from Geneva to Lausanne, the second-largest city on Lake Geneva, and offers activities in every season.

In the summer, rent a lounge chair on the beach and sunbathe, taking refreshing dips in the lake. In the spring and fall take magnificent hikes through the vineyards, or go biking through the mountains. In the winter, you have endless winter sports opportunities in the Alps, including skiing, snowshoeing and even sleigh adventures.

Nyon Tourism Office
Address: Av. Viollier 8, 1260, Nyon
Telephone +41 (0)22 365 66 00

St. Peter's Cathedral (Old Town)

The city of Geneva is stunning and the lake it is situated upon is gorgeous. You'll want to spend time wandering the cobbled streets of Old Town, nestled right on the shore of the lake. Your exploration of the city should begin here, visiting the historic St. Peter's Basilica.

St. Peter's (St. Pierre) Cathedral belongs to the Swiss Reformed Church, and is the church of Protestant reformer John Calvin. In fact, a chair once used by Calvin remains in the church to this day. The history of the church is much older, however, and extensive excavation has revealed ruins and evidence of a site of worship since the Roman Empire. In the late 700's, the church shared the site with 2 other cathedrals, yet St. Peter's is the only one to remain to this day. When you go inside, make sure you take the time to look at the historic pipe organ and various art works. If you're up for a challenge, climb the towers for a breathtaking view over the city.

Address: Place Bourg-Saint-Pierre 1204 Geneva, Switzerland
Telephone: + 41 (0)22 311 75 75

Upon exiting the cathedral, you'll find yourself in Geneva's Old Town. This area of the city is a wonderful place to get lost in the cobbled alleyways, and spend the afternoon browsing small boutiques or sipping coffee at a sidewalk café. You'll want to head to Maison Tavel, which is a living museum dedicated to Geneva's urban history. Almost the entire house is open to the public, and it serves as a great introduction to life in the city.

Address: Rue du Puits-Saint-Pierre 6 1204 Geneva,
Switzerland
Telephone: +41 (0)22 418 37 00

Head to a crossroads just a short walk from the Maison
Tavel to where Rousseau was born on the Grand Rue.
Gaze down the Rue des Granges, parallel to Grand Rue,
at the gorgeous mansions built for Geneva's most affluent
residents in the 1700's. You'll want to cross the street
towards the Alabama Room, where the Geneva
Convention was signed in 1864, and the League of
Nations met for the first time sixty years later.

You can explore the interior of the building, most notably
the sloped ramp used in the place of stairs. Supposedly
this was to accommodate both canons being wheeled up
to the ramparts and particularly lethargic councilors who
preferred to arrive directly to their meeting room by
horseback.

Explore along the Rue du Puits St. Pierre, with its tiny
shops and cafes, and to Rue Calvin to see a large
collection of non-European art works in the Musée
Barbier-Müller at Number 10 Rue Calvin. To get a taste
of one of Switzerland's most noted art collections, you
should spend a few hours in the Musée d'Art et
d'Histoire (The Art and History Museum), on Number 2
Rue Charles Galland. Here you can see work
commissioned for St. Peter's Cathedral in the early 15th
century on the altarpiece by Konrad Witz, which depicts
Jesus and a group of fishermen on Lake Geneva.

Whether you choose to pick a few places of interest and plan your tour of Old Town around them, or you decide to just wander until you happen upon a museum, church, cathedral, or café, at least plan for a long afternoon walking these cobbled streets. You'll want to stay far beyond the sun sets.

United Nations Building

During your visit to Geneva, you have the unique opportunity to visit the second-largest United Nations office (after the United Nations Headquarters in New York City). The United Nations Office in Geneva (UNOG) is located in the stunning "Palais des Nations", built in the 1800's. The Palais is located in the massive Ariana Park, which overlooks the Lake and offers views of Mont Blanc on a clear day. Many member nations contributed to the design of the building, which is said to reflect the stability the UN was aiming for after the widespread destruction of the two World Wars.

While you're here try to see:

- **The Human Rights and Alliance of Civilizations Room**, which is beautifully decorated with art works by Miquel Barceló.
- **The Salle des Pas Perdus**, where you can see a monument that "commemorates the conquest of outer space".
- The place where many significant negotiations have taken place: **The Council Chamber.**

Hundreds of thousands of gifts that have been presented to the Palais and UNOG since its inception.

When planning a tour of the United Nations, keep in mind that this is a working office place, so some corridors or rooms might be closed for meetings. It's best to check the website to make sure on which days the building is open and at which times.

Visitors' Service:
Address: Palais des Nations 14, Avenue de la Paix 1211 Geneva
Tel: +41 (0)22 917 48 96 or +41(0)22 917 45 39

Carouge Neighborhood

Carouge began life in the late 18th century, as a part of the Kingdom of Sardinia. As a result, this tiny suburban area in Geneva has a distinctly Mediterranean feel, from the lively streets to the shade-soaked squares where you can sit and people-watch for hours.

This small annex is separated from Geneva by the River Arve, and seems to be separated by much more. Where Geneva is decidedly Swiss and Alpine, historic and stoic, Carouge is very bohemian, probably not in small part because of the large number of artists and young people living here.

Much of this vibe is earned in part by its history: Carouge was at one time a favorite among Protestants looking to escape at least for an evening the strict laws banning alcohol and dancing in Geneva. Carouge is still busting at the seams with cafes, bars, and nightclubs, and has remained a popular party location for residents and visitors alike. It's an easy river crossing if you use the tram system. It is in fact only a 10-minute ride from the center of Geneva into Carouge.

The first thing you'll notice when entering Carouge is the green shutters on the front of so many of the small three-story houses. The green shutters were part of the original plan of the city when the architects envisioned a city that was a garden in of itself. Inside so many doors and gates, still today, you can see the architects' original vision: each house has a courtyard or a small garden, and the tree-lined streets all lend a garden-feel to this small town. If you want to see a beautiful example of the original architecture, head to Au Vieux Carouge for a taste of delicious Swiss Fondue or more traditional French cuisine. Her you can relax in the cozy interior or the tables sometimes in front of the façade's green shutters when the weather is warm.

Address: Rue Jacques-Dalphin 27, 1227 Carouge, Switzerland
Telephone: +41 (0)22 342 64 98
http://www.auvieuxcarouge.com/

For an unforgettable Swiss Brasserie experience, you should stop by Brasserie la Bourse, which serves traditional brasserie foods such as huge cheese and meat plates and delectable stews made of local rabbit, venison, or beef. This is a cozy venue, tucked away next to a fountain in the center of Carouge, and is very popular with the young residents of the city. Come, grab a table on the sidewalk next to the fountain, and spend hours people-watching the night away.

Address: Place du Marché 7, 1227 Carouge, Switzerland
Telephone: +41 (0)22 300 32 22
http://www.resto.ch/~labourse/index.php/en/

Bastions Park

If you head to the internet, and type in "Geneva, Switzerland" into the search bar, chances are one of the first images that pops up will be the life-sized chess pieces in Bastions Park. Popular with the young, hip Geneva crowd, the Park is filled with activity from the morning until late in the evening, with people jogging, relaxing on the grass or on the benches, or challenging new friends to a game of life-sized chess.

Bastions Park borders Old Town, and there is actually a new wall built right against the old ramparts of the city that delineates the park from the cobbled roads of the Old Town. The rest of the park is lined with trees, some of them remnants of the botanical garden that once stood on this space. The park is a favorite hang-out each day, and one of the best free activities in Geneva. On certain days during the year, however, the park becomes the center of festivities for May Day and a veritable Winter Wonderland around the holidays.

Before your visit, see Geneva's tourism website for special events happening during your visit. Even if you miss the live music and Christmas Trees, however, you'll enjoy your hours spent in Bastions Park, making new friends, or relaxing with old ones. Be sure to brush up on those chess skills.

http://www.geneva.info/parks/

Place du Molarde

No European vacation is complete without a lazy morning spent sipping coffee in a square, people-watching to your heart's content. While in Geneva, you'll want to head into Old Town for the best in people watching, coffee shops, and department stores. Place du Molarde is alive at all hours of the day; during the day, people come to sit, drink coffee, or shop in one of the several department stores or variety of luxury boutique stores.

People also work here, in several of the old office buildings off the square, so don't be surprised if not everyone shares in your sense of laissez-faire during your visit to the square. Avoid the bustling suits, and have a seat, and enjoy the sun as you read a book and enjoy a glass of wine or beer, coffee, or hot chocolate.

The most visible sight in the square is the national monument, built in the late 18th century, that is placed in a huge fountain in the center of the square. Also not to miss is the military tower dominating one of the corners of the square, which in the 1300's was a blockade that protected the port of Molarde.

For an unforgettable café experience, head to number 5 in the Place du Molarde, to the Café du Centre, which is one of the several cafes with outdoor terraces year-round. Not to worry: in the frosty winter months, the tables are usually ensconced in a thick clear plastic tent, and you'll be heated by gas lanterns while cozying up inside. The café also offers food, and is a great place to people-watch, relax, or enjoy a hearty stew or light snack during a break in your touring.

Paquis (Beach, Baths & Ethnic Eateries)

Paquis is a glorious juxtaposition of wealth and charm. On one side of the coin, this is one of the most affluent districts in Geneva, and is located in the center of the city, between the main railway station and Lake Geneva.

Here is where the rich and famous come to live and play, and if your budget is less rigid, you can stay amongst them, in the Beau-Rivage, Hilton, or Bristol, some of the most expensive hotels in the city.

The good news here is that while many of the places to stay are quite expensive, tucked amongst the wealth and carved marble are some inexpensive and free activities, including swimming in the lake from the gorgeous beach at Des Bains des Paquis. You may need to put a little money down to rent a lounge or umbrella, but setting your towel down on the sand is free, and you'll have a spectacular view of the huge fountain in Lake Geneva, the white lighthouse, and the windsurfers and water-skiers all carving their way through the crystal clear waters. The baths on the site are also open year-round, and you'll find several cafes and restaurants to satiate you after an afternoon in the sun, or a Swedish massage at the baths.

Now, the secret to this neighborhood, again, is to duck behind these high-end attractions, and explore the eight square blocks (Rue des Alpes/Rue de Lausanne/Lake Geneva/Parc Mon'Repos) that are filled with restaurants representing cuisine from dozens of countries. Also, you'll want to come here for an incredible (and affordable) shopping experience: make a first stop at Rue des Paquis to scope out the new and used books in the small book traders, make an investment in some locally-crafted silver jewelry, or even buy an authentic oriental rug.

When you're finished shopping, take your pick of the dozens of restaurants in Les Paquis, some Japanese, some Chinese, some Moroccan, to taste authentic ethnic cuisine. It's a good idea to bring along enough cash, as many of the restaurants in this neighborhood still do not accept credit cards.

Your night doesn't end when the check arrives, however. After dinner, head to an authentic Middle Eastern lounge where you can smoke shisha (flavored tobacco) while sipping on wine or tea on huge comfy cushions. The hours will slip away, in a mellow smoky haze, while you relax, chat with the people on neighboring cushions, or tucked away in a corner sharing a romantic evening out.

Plainpalais Flea Market

We all enjoy a good bargain. For an incredible locally-flavored experience, head to the Plainpalais Flea Market, and put on your bargaining hat. You'll need those skills here. Located in the huge open space at 1204 Plainpalais, this space was once used for quarantine for people sick with a contagious illness, but is now used, not only for the famous flea market, but also several times a year for when the circus comes to town, or during Christmas time, when European Christmas Markets pop up in every corner of Geneva.

The flea market is open every Wednesday and Saturday, rain or shine. You can find just about anything you didn't know you wanted here, including a DVD of You Got Mail, or a CD of your favorite Aerosmith album. If you're in the market for some antiques or super-hip 70's or 80's used furniture, this is the place to be, and if you're planning on staying in Geneva for a while, may be a great and cheap way to decorate and furnish your new digs.

Whether you're looking for a bierstein to bring home, or an antique shoe horn, the Plainpalais Flea Market is a perfect place to bargain and browse the day away.

Museum of the Red Cross

Now in the midst of a major expansion project that will greatly expand the museum's exhibit and public spaces, the Museum of the Red Cross is planning a huge re-opening in early 2013. Head to the website to learn more about the expansion, and when the museum will be re-opened.

Even though the new museum will be organized differently than the former lay-out, you can expect a comprehensive photography collection that follows Red Cross and Red Crescent activity in hundreds of disasters around the world. It is a stunning display of humanitarian effort, and a very moving display. follows Red Cross and Red Crescent activity in hundreds of disasters around the world. It is a stunning display of humanitarian effort, and a very moving display.

You can also expect to learn about the founder Henry Dunant, and the history of the importance of Red Cross during the World Wars. An exciting addition to the exhibits will the Geneva Convention, originally written in 1864, and an excellent visual display focused on the importance of the Convention and of Conventions ratified in 1949 that aim to protect innocent civilians during times of conflict.

The museum is very accessible by public transport, and when re-opened will offer a worthy use of a morning or an afternoon marveling at the prolific good deeds done by the Red Cross and Red Crescent since its inception.

http://www.micr.ch/index_e.html

The Saleve (Swiss Alps)

Well, it would be almost a sin to visit Geneva and not at least dip your feet a little in the beauty of the Swiss Alps, rising up around the city. An excellent day-trip from Geneva is The Saleve, easily accessible by public transportation, and such a beautiful Swiss landscape, you may find yourself singing the lines to The Sound of Music's The Hills are Alive! (although that was actually filmed in Salzburg, Austria).

One of the things you should experience is the cable car ride to the top of The Salve, for a sensational view of Mont Blanc and the Swiss Alps. The panoramic views of the mountains will absolutely take your breath away, and even if your trip to The Saleve is limited only to this cable car ride, you'll feel you've had at least a taste of the Alps.

Head to this website for times and days of opening. During extremely windy times, the cable car may not be open, so it's good to check before you go.

http://www.telepheriquedusaleve.com/

In addition to travelling up the cable car and marveling at the views, you might also want to try your hand at parasailing, hiking, or mountain biking, all of which are possible in this area of the Alps. Many of these adventures are family-friendly, so if you have children along, or if flinging yourself off a cliff strapped to a set of nylon wings isn't your cup of tea, you can choose an easier hike, or mountain biking along more level paths. For a great starting point of your trip, head to the Mountain's website to explore all the adventurous possibilities for your trip:

http://www.myswitzerland.com/en/mount-saleve.html

To get to The Saleve, take bus 8, 34, or 41 from the center of Geneva to Veyrier-Ecole. If you are driving, just head straight to Veyrier, right on the French border, to park underneath the cable car.

Recommendations for the Budget Traveller

Places to Stay

While some neighborhoods in Geneva are understandably quite expensive to stay in, you'll be surprised at the hidden gems you'll find to give you a stay you'll never forget. Here are a few.

Hotel Central

This centrally located hotel (about 10 minutes from Old Town) is a great bargain, and a fine place to hang your hat for your visit.

Breakfast can be delivered to your room between 7 am and 9 am. Rooms have a mini-fridge so you can tuck away some chocolates for dessert in bed. The service is warm and personal, and rooms clean and comfortable.

Address: 2, rue de la Rotisserie, Geneva CH-1204, Switzerland
Telephone: +41 (0) 022 818 81 00
http://www.hotelcentral.ch/
Price range: USD 100 – 200

Appart'Hôtel Résidence Dizerens

While the name is a mouthful, the hotel itself is very budget-friendly, and centrally located in Geneva. The guesthouse is actually located on a pedestrian street in the city, tucked away from the traffic of the main streets. Each tiny apartment has its own kitchenette, which makes saving money on meals as easy as pie. Each room has a TV and DVD player, if you simply must spend an evening in. A bonus is the laundry facility located on premises, as well as its location, only about a 10-minute walk from the University of Geneva.

Address: Rue Dizerens 7 Geneva CH-1204, Switzerland
Telephone: +41 (0)22 809 61 11
http://www.apparthotel-residence-dizerens.rooms-easy.com/
Price range: USD 100 – 140

Ibis Geneve Central Gare Hotel

This clean and efficient hotel is perfect for travelling business people interested in fast internet and a central location, as well as tourists more into the polished feel of a chain hotel than a guesthouse. It is located in the city center, right near the Grand Casio, and features a bar in the premises that is open 24/7: perfect for that night-cap before bed after a long day's touring.

Address: Rue Voltaire 10 Geneva CH-1204, Switzerland
Telephone: +41 (0)22 338 20 20
http://www.accorhotels.com/gb/hotel-2154-ibis-geneve-centre-gare/index.shtml

Places to Eat & Drink

Buvette Bains des Paquis

Located in the diverse and charming Paquis neighborhood, this probably is one of the most interesting dining experiences you can have in Switzerland. The Buvette is set in the Bains des Paquis, and is a perfect cherry on top of a day lounging on the beach or in the baths. The restaurant has a small terrace that is open when the weather allows it, and offers superb views of the Jet d'Eau (fountain), water-sports on the Lake, and the Kempinski Hotel.

The "interesting" aspect comes when the clients of the Turkish baths on the premises emerge from the baths naked to head to the decks to warm up in the sun. If this doesn't faze you, you simply must not miss the famous "Champagne Fondue" served from September through April. Reservations are a must for these months, but recommended year-round. No credit cards are accepted here, so be sure to check out the menu online and bring the appropriate amount of cash.

Address: 30 quai du Mont-Blanc, Les Pâquis, Geneva, 1201
Telephone: +41 (0) 227381616
www.buvettedesbains.ch

Le Thé

A day bargaining at the Plainpalais Flea Market is bound to whet your appetite! For a deliciously authentic Asian culinary experience, head to Le Thé, and try the dim sum, tapioca, and delicate shrimp crepes. Even if you're only in the mood for a pot of tea, this restaurant is worth a peek, but if you plan on staying for a meal, then it's advisable to call ahead for a reservation. Once you're finished eating, you may want to walk to 5 Rue des Savoises for the restaurant's own shopping emporium Dragon Art, in case you want to shop for Asian-themed souvenirs or a box of tea to bring home with you. Bring cash, as no credit cards are accepted here.

Address: 65 rue des Bains, Plainpalais, Geneva, 1205
Telephone: +41 079 4367718

Chez Ma Cousine

Your travels will without a doubt bring you into Old Town, and a scrumptious dinner can be found at this charmingly decorated restaurant. However, there is something special about this particular restaurant: they do only three things, and they do them perfectly. For lunch or dinner, you can expect the following: a roast chicken (whole if you are a couple, a half if you are ordering single portions), potatoes, and a crisp salad. That's it. No muss, no fuss. The chicken is roasted to perfection, and at less than 15 Swiss Francs per person, this is certainly a meal you can sink your teeth into. Plus, the people watching here is unparalleled.

Address: 6 place du Bourg-de-Four, Vieille Ville, Geneva, 1204
Telephone: +41 (0)22 3109696
Website: www.chezmacousine.ch

Maison Rouge

You absolutely won't want to miss this unique dining experience, located just North of Carouge, across the river from Geneva. The name means "Red House," and the restaurant is just that: a big, red house. What makes this place so special is that the owner cooks all the dishes himself. Miraculously, while feeding his guests, he will find time to wander out of the kitchen, chat with the guests and make sure everyone's having a good time. A real gem, and a dinner you won't soon forget.

Rue des Noirettes 17, Geneva 1227, Switzerland
+4122 342 00 42
http://www.lamaisonrouge.ch/

Places to Shop

Geneva is a shopper's dream: from huge department stores, to specialty chocolate or clothing boutiques, to the flea markets and seasonal Christmas Markets, there's sure to be something for just about anyone, including the friends and family back home. In Switzerland, expect most stores to be closed on Sundays, and also closed (with the exception of the larger department stores) from 2:00 – 4:00 pm on weekdays. Here are some shopping locations not to miss:

If you are in the market for a Swiss watch, you've come to the right place: the watch industry in Switzerland dates to the 17th century and Geneva is the place to find the perfect one. Head to either **Expace Temps or Bucherer**, located on Rue du Mont Blanc 13and 22, respectively. Even if a new watch is not in your budget for this trip, you can still head to the **Piaget** store at Rue du Rhone 40 for a window-shopping experience you won't soon forget.

A slightly more affordable gift for yourself or loved ones is some prized Swiss chocolate. Of course, you are in Switzerland so really you could stop of at the grocery store or local market for some of the best chocolate you've ever tasted, but here are some other options for a more artisanal chocolate experience.

The Cartier Patisserie Confiserie Chocolaterie, on Route de Suisse 38, is your golden ticket to the best sweets and pastries you could imagine. For over 150 years, the Cartier family has sold chocolates to the residents and visitors of Geneva, and remains a favorite. Plan on sitting down or a few minutes and pairing that chocolate croissant or truffle with a cappuccino or if you're brave, even a cup of molten hot real chocolate, topped with a dollop of whipped cream. Decadence at its best, and one of the city's shining jewels.

http://www.cartier-swiss.ch/

Also a historical chocolate store, **Rohr** is another family-run business that will have your heart fluttering and your mouth watering for more. Head to the Place du Molard, and you'll find Rohr tucked into number 3, offering an excellent respite from a long day's touring.

http://www.rohr.ch/en/

Geneva is a window-shopper's paradise. If you're more into the gazing than the buying, you want to be sure to head to these neighborhoods. Not only do they offer the best shopping opportunities in the city, but it's in these neighborhoods that you'll discover that alongside hiking and skiing, window-shopping is practically a sport in Switzerland. The people watching is sensational, and the restaurants and cafes here are perfect oases when you've reached your shopping (or credit card) limit.

Rue du Mont Blanc: This street, and several streets surrounding it, offer a wide variety of clothing shops and jewelry stores, and is a perfect place to pick up mementos of your vacation, or gifts of Swiss Pocket Knives for your friends back home.

Old Town: You must get lost here to truly appreciate how magical this part of Geneva is. Each twist and turn reveals a small store, a boutique, an artisan's studio and store. What is an extra-special treat is finding one of the dozens of small antique stores, which really should be called museums, as artifacts and art works from the Middle Ages can be bought (at a price) here. Ask the shop owner the history of the piece, and you'll be surprised how excited some owners are to tell you about how they acquired the piece, and what its historical significance is.

Manor Department Store, on Rue Cornavin 6 (+41 (0) 22 909 4699), is one of the largest department stores in Geneva, and is known throughout the country for its variety of clothing collections, electronics, and perfumes. An added treat is the food market, located on the ground floor, which is popular with locals taking a break during the workday.

http://www.manor.ch/

Printed in Great Britain
by Amazon.co.uk, Ltd.,
Marston Gate.